Make It Glorious

T0048183

Transcriptions and Engravings - Ed Kerr
Editors - Rhonda Scelsi & Luke Gambill
Executive Producer - Craig Dunnagan

hosanna! music

A voice of one calling: "In the desert prepare the way for the LORD; make straight in the wilderness a highway for our God." Isaiah 40:3 (NIV)

Prepare Ye The Way

Words and Music by
TOMMY WALKER

make a way____ for the Lord.____

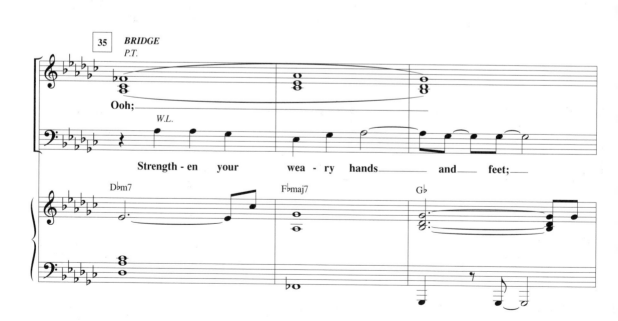

Ooh;

Strength-en your wea-ry hands____ and____ feet;____

10

12

Make a way

Medley options: I Love To Be In Your Presence; Stir Up A Hunger.

Make It Glorious

Words and Music by
TOMMY WALKER

19

20

22

24

Medley options: Hosanna (OLIVER); Blessed Be The Lord (OLIVER).

26

Therefore God exalted him to the highest place and gave him the name that is
above every name. Philippians 2:9 (NIV)

Jesus, We Celebrate Your Fame

Words and Music by
TOMMY WALKER

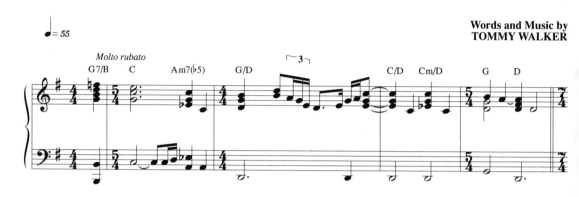

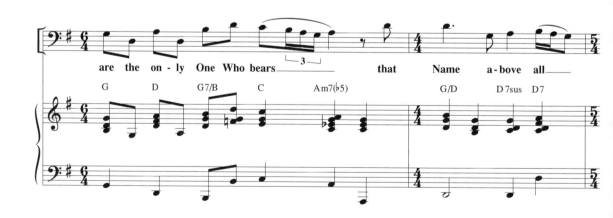

© 2004 Integrity's Praise! Music c/o Integrity Media, Inc., 1000 Cody Road, Mobile, AL 36695
All rights reserved.   Used by Permission. CCLI# 4187804

28

30

32

His great fame we sing.

Medley options: Think About His Love; Redeemer, Savior, Friend.

Praise be to the God and Father of our Lord Jesus Christ! In his great mercy he has given us new birth
into a living hope through the resurrection of Jesus Christ from the dead. 1 Peter 1:3 (NIV)

Heavenly Touch

Words and Music by
TOMMY WALKER

36

filled with such love;_____ O, the mys - ter - y_____

G/B   C   D   G   D

_ how it reach - es deep in me, re -

D/C   G/B   C

stor - ing my___ soul   and mak - ing me

G/D   D   D/C   G/B

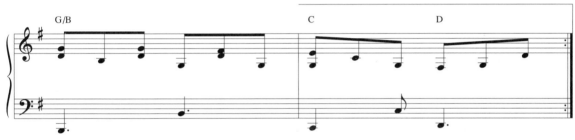

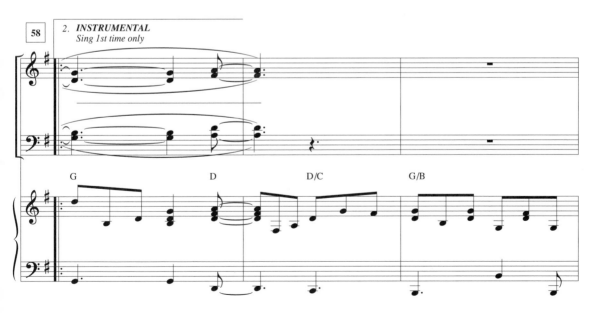

40

42

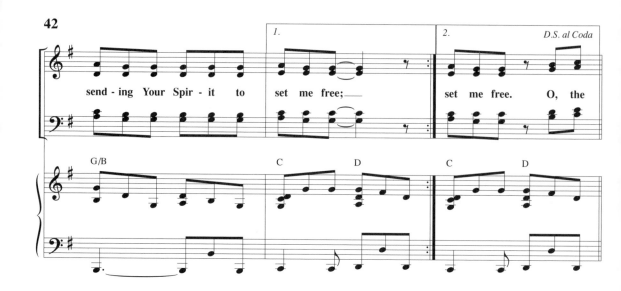

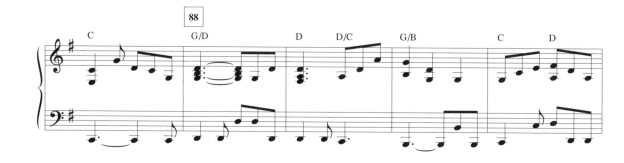

44

Medley options: Shout To The North; He Is Exalted.

Thank You For Loving Me

Words and Music by
TOMMY WALKER

48

50

52

54

Medley options: Never Gonna Stop; I Could Sing Of Your Love Forever.

Exalt the LORD our God and worship at his footstool; he is holy. Psalm 99:5 (NIV)

Just Worship

Words and Music by
TOMMY WALKER

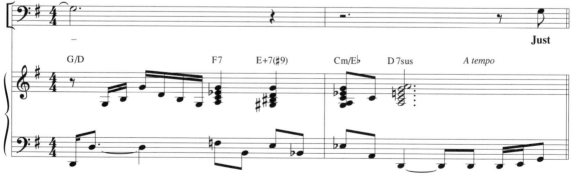

58

60

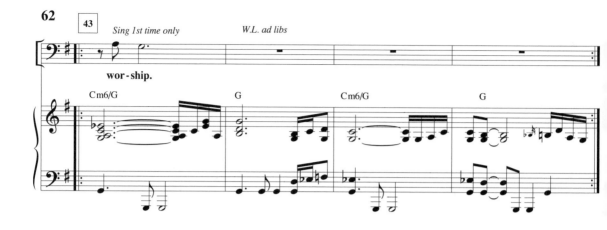

Medley options: Holy Spirit Rain Down; In The Presence.

O LORD God Almighty, who is like you? You are mighty, O LORD, and your faithfulness
surrounds you. Psalm 89:8 (NIV)

This God He Is Our God

Words and Music by
TOMMY WALKER

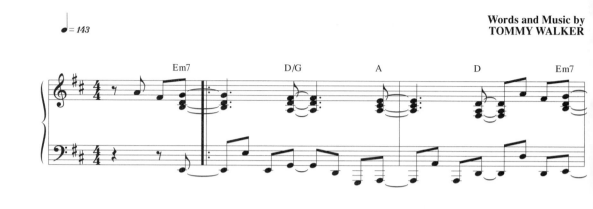

7 VERSE
Ladies

1. Who is the God Who said to the dark-ness let there be light and___
2. This is the God Who came down from Heav-en, said let the chil-dren___

Men

In - vis - i - ble, yet__ ev - er pres - ent,
It is His love that will ev - er hold us

He is the ho - ly
un - til the day we

D/G   Bm7   A   Em7   D/G   Bm7

God   Most   High.
see   His   face.

A   Asus   A

𝄋 **25** *CHORUS*

This God, He__ is our God for - ev - er - more and__ ev -

D   A   Em11   G2

68

70

Medley options: Rise Up And Praise Him; Open Up The Sky.

Optional spoken part:

All: He's the Holy One, the I Am, the Beginning and the End, the infinite, all-powerful, all-knowing, ever-present, invisible, miracle-working God. He's the Creator of the world, the Righteous Judge, the King of kings and the Lord of lords.

Worship Leader: So who is this God?

Praise Team: This God is our God forever and ever. He will be our God even to the end.

All: He's the Lamb of God, the Bread of life, the Firm Foundation, the Bright and Morning Star. His Name is Emmanuel, Redeemer, Wonderful Counselor, the Everlasting Father and the Ancient of Days. He's the Rewarder, the Healer, the Prince of Peace, the Hope of Glory, and He's our soon and coming King.

I am not ashamed of the gospel, because it is the power of God for the salvation of
everyone who believes... Romans 1:16 (NIV)

I'm Not Ashamed

𝅘𝅥 = 110

**Words and Music by
TOMMY WALKER**

Ladies, 2nd time only

1. I'm not a-shamed___ of___ Your love,   not a-shamed___ of___ Your grace,
2. What can I do___ but dance___ and shout;   I have to let___ these prais - es out;

Worship Leader   *Add Men, 2nd time only*

76

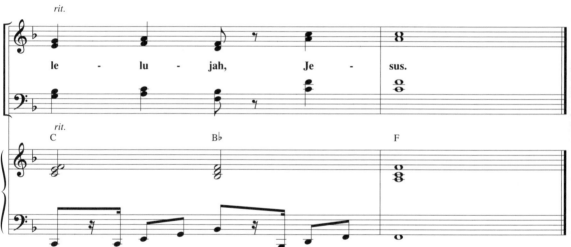

Medley options: Celebrate The Lord Of Love; The Lord Be Magnified.

The name of the LORD is a strong tower; the righteous run to it and are safe. Proverbs 18:10 (NIV)

81

Lord I Run To You

**Words and Music by
TOMMY WALKER**

♩ = 54

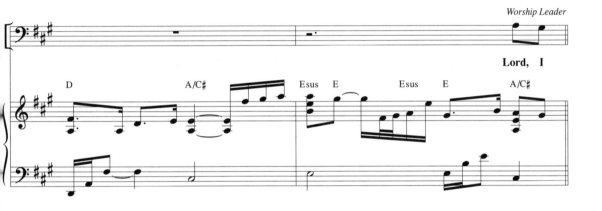

Worship Leader

Lord, I

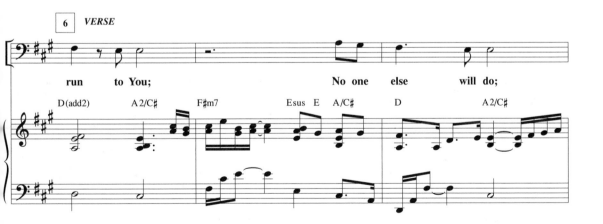

run   to You;   No one   else   will do;

Lord, in trou - bled times, I will

run straight____ to You;____ Though my heart and flesh____ may fail, You're my

ev - er pres - ent help, my tow - er____ of strength, my

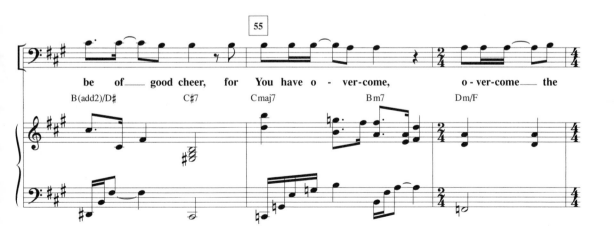

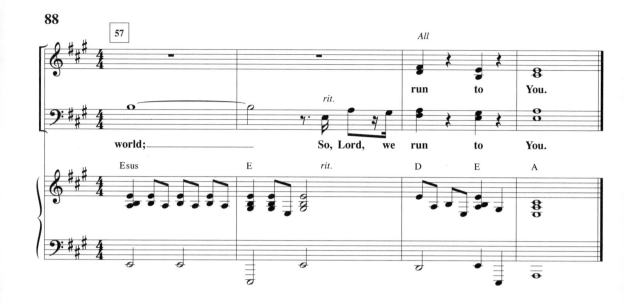

Medley options: There Is None Like You; I Hide Myself In Thee.

Lord, you have been our dwelling place throughout all generations. Psalm 90:1 (NIV)

89

Dwelling Place

Words and Music by
TOMMY WALKER

90

Medley options: Redeemer, Savior, Friend; Lay My Life Down.

My spirit rejoices in God my Savior. Luke 1:47 (NIV)

95

Hallelujah, What A Savior

Words and Music by PHILLIP P. BLISS
Arranged by TOMMY WALKER

98

100

Medley options: Above All; In Your Presence O God.

The grass withers and the flowers fall, but the word of our God stands forever. Isaiah 40:8 (NIV)

101

Your Word Will Be The Last Word

Words and Music by
TOMMY WALKER

Guitar Sheets

Make It Glorious (1 of 2)

Tommy Walker

INTRO
Bm7(b5)   E7   Am7   D7#9   Gm7   Gm7/C   F7
   Make it glori- ous,   make it   wonder-ful
(1st & 2nd ending)
Bm7(b5)   E7   Am7   D7#9   Gm7   Gm7/C   F   Gm7   G#dim7   F/A
   Make it excel- lent, the praises of our   King

(Repeat)

(3rd ending)
Bm7(b5)   E7   Am7   D7#9   Gm7   Gm7/C   F
   Make it excel- lent, the praises of our   King

VERSE
F   F/A   Eb/Bb Bb   F   F/A   Eb/Bb Bb   Dm7   G7   Bbm   Bbm6
   Make it glor- ious,   make it won- derful, the   praises of our King
F   F/A   Eb/Bb Bb   Dm7   G7
  Make it pas- sionate, given from our hearts
Bb2   C7sus   F
Sing prais- es to our King
F   F/A   Eb/Bb Bb   F   F/A   Eb/Bb Bb   Dm7   G7   Bbm   Bbm6
   Make it ex- cellent, make it beau- tiful, the   praises of our King
F   F/A   Eb/Bb Bb   Dm7   G7
   Let Him hear   how much we really thank Him
Bb2   C7sus   F
Sing prais- es to our King.

CHORUS
Gm7   C   Gm7   C
Shout with joy to our God
Gm7   C   C#dim7   Dm7   C#dim7   F/C
All the earth, give glory to His Name
F   C   Gm7   C
He de- serves nothing less
(1st ending)
C   Gm7   F/A   F/Bb   Bb2   Bm7(b5)   E7   Am7   D7#9
Than our hearts and souls, our ver-   y   best
Gm7   Gm7/C   F
(Repeat Verse & Chorus)

Make It Glorious (2 of 2)

(2nd ending)
C   Gm7   F/A   F/Bb   Bb2
Than our hearts and souls, our ver-   y

INSTRUMENTAL
Bm7(b5)   E7   Am7   D7aug(#9)   Gm7   C7   Eb/F   F
best
Bm7(b5)   E7   Am7   D7aug(#9)   Gm7   Bb/C

F   Gm7   G#dim7   F/A   Bm7(b5)

BRIDGE
Bm7(b5) E7   Am7   D7(#9)   Gm7   C7   Eb/F   F
        Make it glori-   ous,   make it wonder- ful
(1st, 2nd & 3rd endings)
Bm7(b5)   E7   Am7   Daug7(#9)   Gm7   Bb/C F   Gm7   G#dim7   F/A
        Make it excel-   lent, the   praises   of our King
(Repeat)

(4th ending)
Bm7(b5)   E7   Am7   Daug7(#9)   Gm7   Bb/C F
        Make it excel-   lent, the   praises   of our King

CHORUS
F   C   Gm7   C
Shout with joy to our God
Gm7   C   C#dim7   Dm7   C#dim7   F/C
All the earth, give glory to His Name
F   C   Gm7   C
He de- serves nothing less
C   Gm7   F/A   F/Bb Bb2   Bm7(b5)   E7   Am7   D7#9
Than our hearts and souls, our ver-   y   best
Gm7   Gm7/C   F

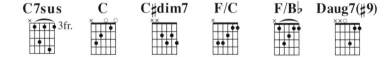

Jesus, We Celebrate Your Fame (1 of 2)

Tommy Walker

INTRO
```
G7/B   C   Am7(b5)   G/D   C/D   Cm/D   G   D
```

VERSE 1
```
G        D    G7/B   C         G/D           Am7    D7/F#
Jesus, Jesus, Jesus,    Jesus, we celebrate Your fame
      G    D    G7/B   C  Am7(b5) G/D    D7      C/G   Cm/G   G   D7sus
You are the only One Who bears    that  Name a-bove all names
G        D         G7      C         G/D           Am7    D/F#
God made flesh You came to earth when a star announced Your glorious birth
      G         D       G        C         G/D    D       Gsus   G/A   A
You shed Your blood and then were raised, now all Heaven sings Your praise
```

VERSE 2
```
D        A    D7/F# G         D/A           Em7    A7
Jesus, Jesus, Jesus,   Jesus, now the nations sing Your song
      Bm7      A/C#   D    G        D/A    A7     Dsus   D
Even now there's millions far and wide lifting up Your Name on high
```

CHORUS
```
D        G    Em7   Bm7      G    E/G#   A
Hallelu- jah, hallelu- jah, hallelu- jah to the King
D        G    A#dim7 Bm7   Bm7/A   G          Asus  A   D
Hallelu- jah to our Sav- ior,   it's of     His great fame  we sing
D        G    Em7   Bm7      G    E/G#   A
Hallelu- jah, hallelu- jah, hallelu- jah to the King
D        G    A#dim7 Bm7   Bm7/A   G          Asus  A   D   Bb7sus   Bb7
Hallelu- jah to our Sav- ior,   it's of     His great fame  we sing
```

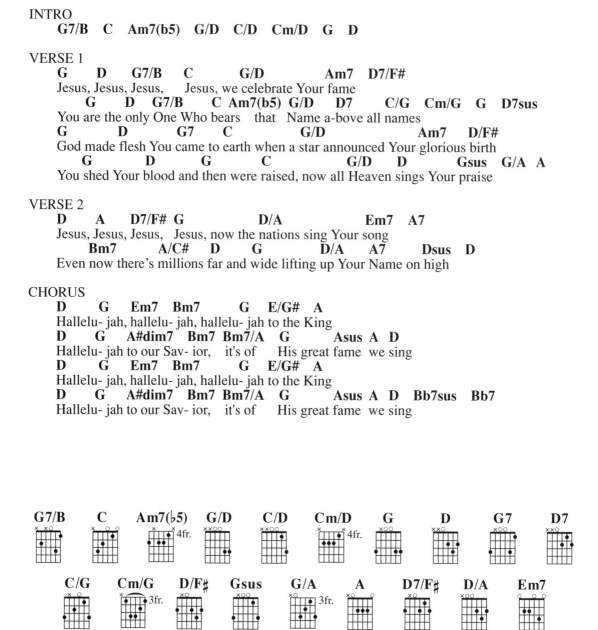

Jesus, We Celebrate Your Fame (2 of 2)

VERSE 3

Eb   Bb   Eb7/G Ab   Eb/Bb   Fm7   Bb7
Jesus, Jesus, Jesus,   Jesus, all history pro- claims
    Cm7   Bb/D Eb   Ab   Eb/Bb   Bb7sus   Ebsus   Eb
The earth has never been the same since You showed the world Your grace

VERSE 4

Eb   Bb   Eb7/G Ab   Eb/Bb   Fm7   Bb7
Jesus, Jesus, Jesus,   Jesus, soon every knee will bow
    Cm7   Bb/D Eb   Ab   Eb/Bb Bb7sus   Ebsus   Eb
We'll crown You Lord and King of kings and then all the   world will sing

CHORUS

Eb   Ab Fm7 Cm7   Ab F/A   Bb
Hallelu- jah, hallelu- jah, hallelu- jah to the King
Eb   Ab Bdim7 Cm7 Cm7/Bb Ab   Bb7sus Bb   Eb
Hallelu- jah to our Sav- ior, it's of   His great fame   we   sing
Eb   Ab Fm7 Cm7   Ab F/A   Bb
Hallelu- jah, hallelu- jah, hallelu- jah to the King
Eb   Ab Bdim7 Cm7 Cm7/Bb Ab   Bb7sus Bb   Eb
Hallelu- jah to our Sav- ior, it's of   His great fame   we   sing

INSTRUMENTAL

Bb7 Bdim7 Cm7 Eb7 Ab F7/A Bb Bb7sus Bb
(1st & 2nd endings)
G7/B Cm7 Cm7/Bb Ab Bb7sus Bb

(3rd ending)
G7/B Cm7 Cm7/Bb Ab Bb7sus Bb Ebsus Eb

CHORUS

Eb   Ab Fm7 Cm7   Ab F/A   Bb
Hallelu- jah, hallelu- jah, hallelu- jah to the King
Eb   Ab Bdim7 Cm7 Cm7/Bb Ab   Bb7sus Bb   Eb
Hallelu- jah to our Sav- ior, it's of   His great fame   we   sing
(Repeat twice)

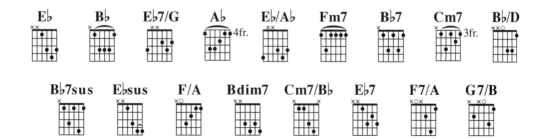

Heavenly Touch (1 of 2)

Tommy Walker

INTRO
    G D D/C G/B C D

VERSE 1
    Em7   **Dsus** **D** **A/C#** **B/D#**   **B7/E** **Em7** **D/E** **Em7** **D**
    Heaven's great mys-   tery   how the God of e- ter-   ni- ty
                C **G/B**   **Am7**
    Reaches down far from worlds un- known
    G/B   **C** **A/C#**   **Dsus** **D** **B7sus**   **B**
    To the human soul making His love in us known
    Em7   **Dsus** **D**   **A/C#** **B/D#**   **B7/E** **Em7** **D/E** **Em7**
    Heaven's great blessing received   is a God full of mer- cy   so   free
    D   **C** **G/B**   **Am7**
    Reaching out throughout time and through space
    G/B   **C**   **A/C#**   **Dsus**   **D**   **C/E**   **D/F#**
    To the human race re- vealing His peace and His grace

CHORUS
    D/F# **G**   **D** **D/C**   **G/B**   **C**
    O the wonder of   His heavenly touch
    G/D   **D** **D/C** **G/B**   **C** **D**
    Filled with such hope   filled with such love
       G   **D** **D/C**   **G/B**   **C**
    O the myste- ry   how it reaches deep in me
       G/D   **D** **D/C** **G/B**   **C** **D**   **G** **D** **D/C** **G/B** **C** **D**
    Re- storing my soul   and making me ev- er whole

VERSE 2
    Em7   **Dsus** **D** **A/C#** **B/D#**   **B7/E** **Em7** **D/E** **Em7**
    Heaven's great his-   tory   shows a God full of kind- ness   and strength
    D   **C** **G/B**   **Am7**
    Raining down on the hardest of hearts
    G/B   **C**   **A/C#**   **Dsus** **D**   **B7sus**   **B**
    Piercing through all the dark with healing and light from a- far

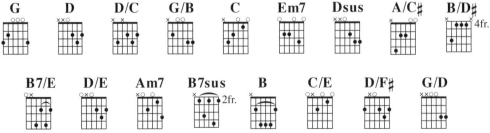

Heavenly Touch (2 of 2)

VERSE 2 (continued)
```
   Em7          Dsus  D      A/C#  B/D#              B7/E  Em7  D/E  Em7
   Heaven's great gift to   the earth        was our Savior our Lord's hum- ble  birth
   D       C  G/B                   Am7
   He came down from His throne up above
   G/B            C  A/C#     Dsus  D   C/E  D/F#
   To be born here in us giving His unend- ing love
```

CHORUS
```
   D/F# G       D D/C     G/B         C
   O the wonder of       His heavenly touch
   G/D            D D/C  G/B           C  D
   Filled with such hope      filled with such love
        G      D D/C      G/B            C
   O the myste- ry      how it reaches deep in me
        G/D       D D/C   G/B        C  D     G
   Re- storing my soul    and making me ev- er whole
```

INSTRUMENTAL
```
   G  D  D/C  G/B  C  G/D  D  D/C  G/B  C  D
```
   (Repeat)

BRIDGE
```
   G               D        D/C G/B          C
   All I wanna do is thank You, Lord, all I wanna do is praise You, Lord for
   G/D        D       D/C  G/B              C       D
   Touching me, loving me and sending Your Spirit to set me free
```
   (Repeat 4 times)

CHORUS
```
   D/F# G       D D/C     G/B         C
   O the wonder of       His heavenly touch
   G/D            D D/C  G/B           C  D
   Filled with such hope      filled with such love
        G      D D/C      G/B            C
   O the myste- ry      how it reaches deep in me
        G/D       D D/C   G/B        C  D     G  D  D/C  G/B  C
   Re- storing my soul    and making me ev- er whole
   G/D  D  D/C  G/B  C  D
```

BRIDGE
```
   G               D        D/C G/B          C
   All I wanna do is thank You, Lord, all I wanna do is praise You, Lord for
   G/D        D       D/C  G/B              C       D
   Touching me, loving me and sending Your Spirit to set me free
```
   (Repeat twice)

```
   G  D  D/C  G/B  C  G/D  D  D/C  G/B  C  D
```
   (Repeat as desired)
```
   G
```

Thank You For Loving Me (1 of 2)

Tommy Walker

INTRO
   G

VERSE 1
```
     G                        D/F#
     What love the Father has lavished on us
     D/F#              Em7      Em7/D   C              Dadd4/C
     That we should be called His sons and daugh- ters, pre- cious in His sight
              G            D/F#
     Greater love this world has never seen when He hung on that tree
     D/F# Em      Em7/D           C              Dsus  D
     O, why did He do such a thing for dirt- y sinners like you and   me
```

CHORUS
```
     D  G  D/F#                Em         G/D                  C
     O God, thank You for loving me when on the cross You made history
     C      G/B         C              Dsus  D
     Lord, You died for me, forev- er my praise will go to   Thee
     D  G  D/F#                Em         G/D                  C
     O God, thank You for choosing me to be Your child and bear Your Name
     C  G/B         C          Dsus     D
     O Je- sus, I will nev- er cease to sing Your praise
```

VERSE 2
```
           G                      D/F#                   Em7
     Your love is patient and humble and kind, it's greater than all my sin
        Em7/D           C              Dsus  D
     It al-   ways protects and trusts and hopes and will have no   end
     D      G                 D/F#                   Em7
     It's Your love that lifted me up from the depths, set my feet on a solid rock
        Em7/D              C                Dsus  D
     With a firm place to stand, Lord, I al- ways will trust in Your lov- ing   hand
```

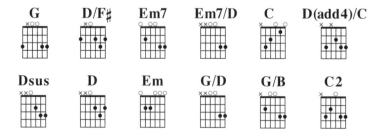

Thank You For Loving Me (2 of 2)

CHORUS
```
    D   G  D/F#              Em        G/D             C
O God, thank You for loving me when on the cross You made history
    C       G/B          C              Dsus D
Lord, You died for me, forev- er my praise will go to    Thee
    D   G  D/F#              Em        G/D             C
O God, thank You for choosing me to be Your child and bear Your Name
    C  G/B        C            Dsus     D
O Je- sus, I will nev- er cease to sing Your praise
```

BRIDGE
```
    D     C2               Dsus  D
How wide, how long, how high, how deep
    D     C2            Dsus  D
How end- less is Your love for   me
    D     C2               Dsus  D
How wide, how long, how high, how deep
    D     C2           Dsus  D
How endless is Your love for me
```
(Repeat)

CHORUS
```
    D   G  D/F#              Em        G/D             C
O God, thank You for loving me when on the cross You made history
    C       G/B          C            Dsus  D
Lord, You died for me, forev- er my praise will go to    Thee
    D   G  D/F#              Em        G/D             C
O God, thank You for choosing me to be Your child and bear Your Name
```
(1st ending)
```
    C  G/B        C            Dsus  D
O Je- sus, I will nev- er cease to sing Your praise
```
(Repeat)

(2nd ending)
```
    C  G/B        C            Dsus       D
O Je- sus, I will nev- er cease to sing Your praise
```

```
    D                   G  D/F#                Em7
Thank You for loving me,    thank You for loving me
```

```
    C                   G  D/F#                Em7
Thank You for loving me,    thank You for loving me
```
(Repeat 3 times)
```
    C               G
Thank You for loving me
```

Just Worship (1 of 2)

Tommy Walker

CHORUS
>   C#m7(b5) Cm6   G/B   Bm7(b5)/F
Just worship,   Lord, I worship You
>   Eaug7(#9) Am7   Cm6
Just want to   honor You
>   Am7(b5) G/D   F7   Eaug7(#9)   Cm/Eb   D7sus
How my heart longs for You

VERSE 1
>   Cm6/G G   Em/B   B7
Just wor-   ship that's all I want to do
>   F#dim7/E Em   G/A   A
Is wor-   ship, give my heart and soul to You
>   C   G/B
To be lost in Your presence and found in Your love
>   Am7   D7sus   D
Letting all things fade away I set my eyes on things a- bove
>   Cm6/G G   F#7sus   B7(b5)   B7
And just wor-   ship I bow before Your throne
>   F#dim7/E Em   G/A   A
And wor-   ship how my heart longs for You a- lone
>   C   G/B
To be lost in Your presence and found in Your love
>   Am7   D7sus   D
Letting all things fade away I set my eyes on things a- bove

CHORUS
>   D   C   G/B   Am7   Em7   D
And just worship, Lord, I worship You
>   C   G/B   Am7   D7sus
Just want to honor You, how my heart longs for You

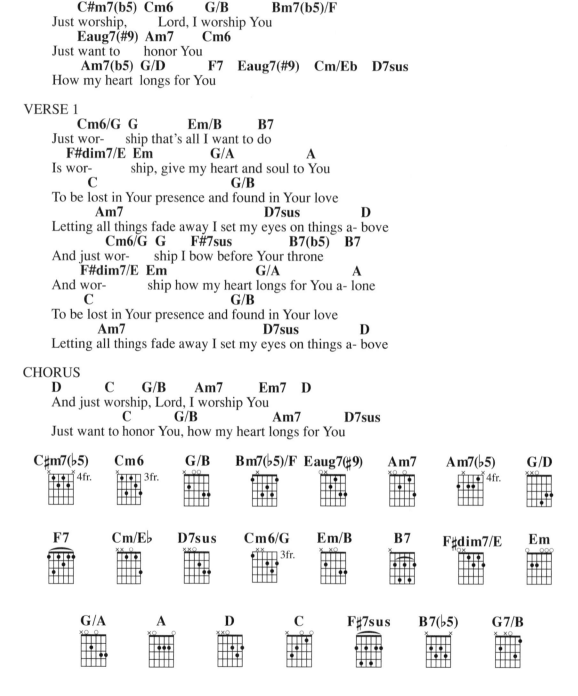

Just Worship (2 of 2)

VERSE 2

      Cm6/G G   **Em/B**   **B7**
To just wo-   ship when I don't know what to do
      F#dim7/E Em   **G/D**   **A**
I'll just wor-   ship casting all my cares on You
      C   **G/B**
To be lost in Your presence and found in Your love
      Am7   **D7sus**   **D**
Letting all things fade away I set my eyes on things a- bove
      Cm6/G G   **F#7sus**   **B7(b5)**   **B7**
And just wor-   ship I bow before Your throne
      F#dim7/E Em   **G/A**   **A**
And wor-   ship how my heart longs for You a- lone
      C   **G/B**
To be lost in Your presence and found in Your love
      Am7   **D7sus**   **D**
Letting all things fade away I set my eyes on things a- bove to just

CHORUS

      C#m7(b5)   **Cm6**   **G/B**   **F7**   **Eaug7(#9)**
Worship,   Lord, I worship You
(1st & 2nd endings)
             Am7   **Cm/Eb**   **G/D**   **F7**   **Eaug7(#9)**   **Cm/Eb**   **D7sus**
Just want to honor You, how my heart longs for You
(Repeat Chorus)

(3rd ending)
             Am7   **Cm/Eb**   **G/D**
Just want to honor You, how my heart longs for You
F7   **Eaug7(#9)**   **Cm/Eb**   **D7sus**
                           O, to just

Cm6/G   **G**   **Cm6/G**   **G**   **Cm6/G**   **G**   **Cm6/G**   **G**
worship

Cm6/G   **G**
All I wanna do, all I wanna do is wor- ship You
Cm6/G   **G**
All I wanna do, all I wanna do is wor- ship You
(Repeat 2 times)

This God He Is Our God (1 of 2)

Tommy Walker

INTRO
Em7   D/G   A   D   Em7   D/G   A   D
(Repeat)

VERSE 1
Em7   D/G   Bm7   A
Who is the God Who said to the darkness
Em7   D/G   Bm7   A
Let there be light and there was light
Em7   D/G Bm7   A
Who is the God Who made the heavens
Em7   D/G   A   D
The sun and moon the stars and sky
Em7 D/G   Bm7   A   Em7 D/G   Bm7 A
He is   One Who's like no other, omni- potent and O, so wise
Em7   D/G Bm7 A
Invis-   ible yet ever- present
Em7 D/G   Bm7   A   Asus   A
He is the holy God Most High

CHORUS
D   A   Em11   G2   A7sus
This God He is our God for- evermore and ever   more
D   A   Em11   G2   A7sus
He'll be our guiding light from now until the end of time
D   A   Em11   G2   A7sus
This God He is our God for- evermore and ever   more
D   A   Em11   G2   A7sus
He'll be our guiding light from now until the end of time
Em7   D/G   A   D   Em7   D/G   A   D
Em7   D/G   A   D   Em7   D/G   A   D

VERSE 2
Em7   D/G   Bm7   A
This is the God Who came down from Heaven
Em7   D/G   Bm7   A
Said let the children come to me
Em7   D/G   Bm7   A
He healed the sick and walked on water
Em7   D/G   A   D
He con- quered death to set us free

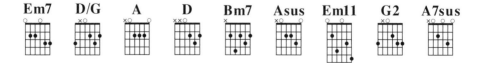

This God He Is Our God (2 of 2)

VERSE 2 (continued)
Em7 D/G   Bm7   A
He is the One Who's always loved us
Em7   D/G   Bm7   A
E-   ven when we've walked a- way
Em7 D/G   Bm7 A
It is   His love that will ever hold us
Em7 D/G   Bm7   A   Asus   A
Until   the day we see His face

CHORUS
D   A   Em11   G2   A7sus
This God He is our God for- evermore and ever   more
D   A   Em11   G2   A7sus
He'll be our guiding light from now until the end of time
D   A   Em11   G2   A7sus
This God He is our God for- evermore and ever   more
D   A   Em11   G2   A7sus
He'll be our guiding light from now until the end of time

BRIDGE
Em7 D/G A   D   Em7 D/G A   D
Halle- lu-   jah,   halle- lu-   jah
Em7 D/G A   D   Em7 D/G A   D
Halle- lu-   jah,   halle- lu-   jah

INSTRUMENTAL
Em7   D/G   A   D   Em7   D/G   A   D
(Repeat as desired)

CHORUS
D   A   Em11   G2   A7sus
This God He is our God for- evermore and ever   more
D   A   Em11   G2   A7sus
He'll be our guiding light from now until the end of time
D   A   Em11   G2   A7sus
This God He is our God for- evermore and ever   more
D   A   Em11   G2   A7sus
He'll be our guiding light from now until the end of time
(Repeat)

Em7 D/G A   D   Em7 D/G A   D
Halle- lu-   jah,   halle- lu-   jah
Em7 D/G A   D   Em7 D/G A   D
Halle- lu-   jah,   halle- lu-   jah

I'm Not Ashamed (1 of 2)

Tommy Walker

INTRO
    F Bb C Bb F Bb C Bb
    (Repeat)

VERSE 1
    F   Bb   C   Bb   F
    I'm not ashamed of Your love, not ashamed of Your grace
    F   Bb   C   Bb   F
    Not ashamed of the cross, not ashamed of Your Word
    F   Bb   C   Bb   F
    From the highest mountain top to the lowest valley low
    F   Bb   C   Bb
    I'll shout Your Name until the whole world knows

CHORUS
    F Bb   Gm7   C
    Je- sus, You're my Master and my King
    F Bb   Gm7   C
    Je- sus, You're my Lord, my everything
    Dm7 Bb F/A   Gm7   C
    Je- sus,   it's Your blood that made me clean
    F   Bb   C Bb
    Hal- lelu- jah, hal- lelu- jah
    F Bb   Gm7   C
    Je- sus, You're my Master and my King
    F Bb   Gm7   C
    Je- sus, You're my Lord, my everything
    Dm7 Bb F/A   Gm7   C
    Je- sus,   it's Your blood that made me clean
    F   Bb   C Bb
    Hal- lelu- jah, hal- lelu- jah

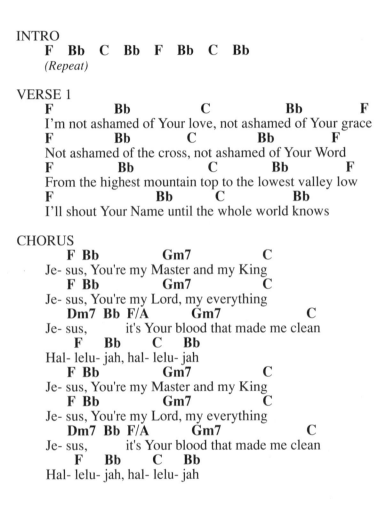

F   Bb   C   Gm7 3fr.   Dm7   F/A

I'm Not Ashamed (2 of 2)

VERSE 2
```
    F         Bb           C           Bb            F
What can I do but dance and shout, I have to let these praises out
    F         Bb          C          Bb             F
I once was lost and O so bound by Your grace I have been found
    F         Bb              C               Bb          F
And if the world can scream and shout for earthly temporary things
    F    Bb          C        Bb
I can give my loudest praise to Thee
```

CHORUS
```
     F Bb          Gm7           C
Je- sus, You're my Master and my King
     F Bb          Gm7           C
Je- sus, You're my Lord, my everything
    Dm7  Bb  F/A      Gm7                 C
Je- sus,       it's Your blood that made me clean
       F    Bb    C    Bb
Hal- lelu- jah, hal- lelu- jah
(Repeat)
```

INSTRUMENTAL
```
F  Bb  C  Bb  F  Bb  C  Bb
(Repeat)
```

BRIDGE
```
F    Bb  C  Bb  F  Bb  C  Bb
Hal-  le- lu- jah, hal- le- lu-  jah
F    Bb  C  Bb  F  Bb  C  Bb
Hal-  le- lu- jah, hal- le- lu- jah
```

CHORUS
```
     F Bb          Gm7           C
Je- sus, You're my Master and my King
     F Bb          Gm7           C
Je- sus, You're my Lord, my everything
    Dm7  Bb  F/A      Gm7                 C
Je- sus,       it's Your blood that made me clean
(1st & 2nd ending)
       F    Bb    C    Bb
Hal- lelu- jah, hal- lelu- jah
(Repeat Chorus)

(3rd ending)
       F    Bb    C    Bb     F    Bb     C    Bb
Hal- lelu- jah, hal- lelu- jah, Hal- lelu- jah, hal- lelu- jah
       F    Bb    C    Bb     F    Bb     C    Bb     F
Hal- lelu- jah, hal- lelu- jah, Hal- lelu- jah, hal- lelu- jah, Je- sus
```

Lord I Run To You (1 of 2)

Tommy Walker

INTRO
    A/C#   D   A2/C#   F#m7   Esus   E   A2/C#   D   A/C#   Esus   E   Esus   E

VERSE 1
    A/C#   D(add2)   A2/C#   F#m7   Esus   E
    Lord, I run to   You
    A/C#   D   A2/C#   Esus   E   Esus   E
    No one else will do
    A/C#   D   A/C#   B(add2)/D#   E
    Lord, in troubled times I will run straight to You
             Dm6/F   A/E   B(add2)/D#   C#7
    Though my heart and flesh may fail You're my ever present   help
        Cmaj7   Bm7   Dm/F   Esus   E
    My tower of strength, my portion ever- more

VERSE 2
    A/C#   D(add2)   A2/C#   F#m7   Esus   E
    Lord, I run to   You
    A/C#   D   A2/C#   Esus   E   Esus   E
    No one else will do
    A/C#   D   A/C#   B(add2)/D#   E
    Lord, You said we'd face   trouble, pain and fear
        Dm6/F   A/E   B(add2)/D#   C#7
    But to be of good cheer,   be of good for cheer
        Cmaj7   Bm7   Dm/F   Esus   E
    For You have over- come, overcome the world

CHORUS
    Dmaj9   A/C#   F#m7   A/E   E
    I lift my eyes up   to the moun- tains
    Dmaj9   A/C#   F#m7   E   A
    Where does my help come from, it comes from You, Lord
    Dmaj9   A/C# F#m7   A/E   E
    You are the Maker   of earth and heav- en
    (1st ending)
    Bm7   A/D   Esus   E   B/D#   E
    And there is nothing that's too hard for You   (so, Lord, we)
    (Repeat Verse 2 & Chorus)

Lord I Run To You (2 of 2)

(2nd ending)
Bm7   A/D   Esus   E   A/C#
And there is nothing that's too hard for You, Lord

CHORUS
Dmaj9 A/C# F#m7 A/E   E
I lift my eyes up   to the moun- tains
Dmaj9   A/C#   F#m7   E   A
Where does my help come from, it comes from You, Lord
Dmaj9   A/C# F#m7   A/E   E
You are the Maker   of earth and heav- en
Bm7   A/D   Esus   E B/D#   E
And there is nothing that's too hard for You

E   Esus   E   Esus   E   Esus   E   Esus   E

VERSE 2
    A/C#   D(add2) A2/C# F#m7 Esus E
So, Lord, I run to   You
A/C#   D   A/C# Esus   E
No one else will do
A/C#   D   A/C#   B(add2)/D#   E
Lord, You said we'd face   trouble, pain and fear
        Dm6/F   A/E   B(add2)/D#   C#7
But to be of good cheer,   be of good for cheer
        Cmaj7   Bm7 Dm/F   Esus   E
For You have over- come, overcome the world
                    D   E   A
So, Lord, we run to You

Dwelling Place (1 of 2)

Tommy Walker

INTRO
G/B   D/E   A   G/B

VERSE
G/B   Dsus D   A/C# Bm7   D/G   D/F#
God of glo- ry, God of won- der, God of beau- ty
                        D/G   A7sus
You reign through all eternity
      A   Dsus D   F#m7   Bm7
Be- fore the moun- tains or the earth had been formed
      D/G   A7sus A Dsus D
You were our ever- last- ing Lord

CHORUS
D   A F#m7   D/F# G   D
You've been our home,   You've been our shelter safe
            A/E E F#m7 D/F# G   D
For young and old   to gener- ations past
            G C/G G   C G/B Am7 G
We stand in awe   of a God   so   great
            D A/C#   A#dim7 Bm7   E
We stand in thanks for Your faithfulness
(1st ending)
  G   A7sus A7 Dsus D A7sus
O Lord, You've been our dwell- ing place
(Repeat Verse & Chorus)

(2nd ending)
  G   A7sus A7 Dsus Dsus/C B7sus
O Lord, You've been our dwell- ing place

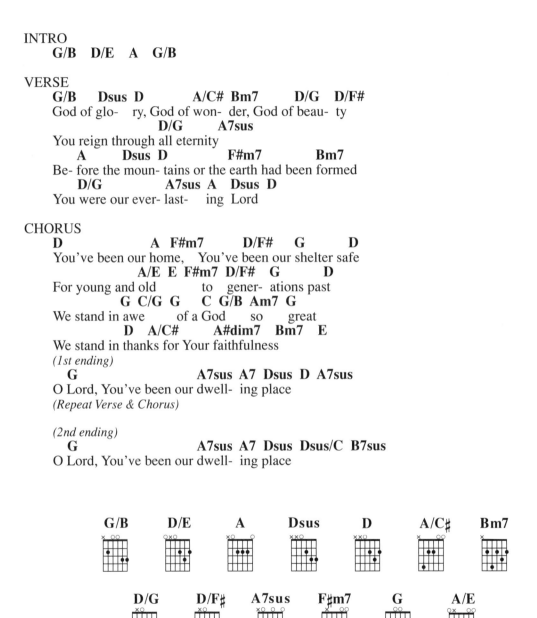

Dwelling Place (2 of 2)

VERSE

B7sus Esus E   **B/D# C#m7**   **A**   **E/G#**
God of glo-   ry, God of won- der, God of beau- ty
               E/A   **B7sus**
You reign through all eterni- ty
          Esus E   **G#m7**   **C#m7**
Before the moun- tains or the earth had been formed
    E/A   **B7sus B Esus E**
You were our ever- last- ing Lord

CHORUS

   E   **B G#m7**   **E/G#**   **A**   **E**
You've been our home,   You've been our shelter safe
           B/F# F# G#m7 E/G#   **A**   **E**
For young and old   to   gener- ations past
      A D/A A   **D A/C# Bm7 A**
We stand in awe   of a God   so   great
       E B/D#   **B#dim7 C#m7**   **F#**
We stand in thanks for Your faithfulness
(1st ending)
  A   **B7sus B7 Esus E**
O Lord, You've been our dwell- ing place
(Repeat Chorus)

(2nd ending)
  A   **B7sus B7 C#m**   **E/F#**   **F#**
O Lord, You've been our dwell- ing place
  A   **B7sus G#/B# C#m**   **E/F#**   **F#**
O Lord, You've been our dwell- ing   place
  A   **E/B**   **B**
O Lord, You've been our dwell- ing
Esus E E/G# A B7sus B E
Place

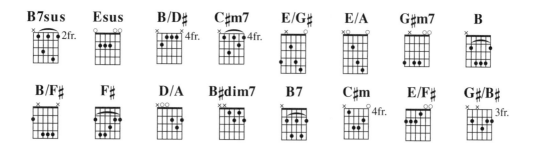

Hallelujah, What A Savior (1 of 2)

Phillip P. Bliss

INTRO
    C/G   G   C/G

VERSE 1
    G   G/B   Em7   D   C   G/B   D/A A   D
    Man of sorrows, what a name for the Son of God Who came
    G   G/B   Em7   C   G/D   D   D/C C
    Ruined sinners to re-   claim, halle- lu-   jah, what a Sav- ior
    G   G/B   Em7   D   C   G/B   D/A   A   D
    Bearing shame and scoffing rude, in my place con- demned He   stood
    G   G/B   Em7   C   G/D   D   D/C C   D
    Sealed my pardon with His blood, halle- lu-   jah, what a Sav- ior

CHORUS
    D   G   D   D/C   C
    Halle- lu- jah, halle- lu-   jah
           G   D   D/C   C
    Halle- lu-   jah, what a Sav- ior
    D   G   D   D/C   C
    Halle- lu- jah, halle- lu-   jah
           G   D   D/C   C
    Halle- lu-   jah, what a Sav- ior

VERSE 2
    G   G/B   Em7   D   C   G/B   D/A A   D
    Guilty, vile and helpless we, spotless Lamb of God was He
    G   G/B   Em7   C   G/D   D   D/C C
    Full of torment, can it be, halle- lu-   jah, what a Sav- ior
    G   G/B   Em7   D   C   G/B   D/A A   D
    Lifted up was He to die, it is finished was His cry
    G   G/B   Em7   C   G/D   D   D/C C   D
    Now in heaven ex- alted   high, halle- lu-   jah, what a Sav- ior

This arrangement © 2004 Integrity's Praise! Music

Hallelujah, What A Savior (2 of 2)

CHORUS
```
    D     G   D       D/C  C
Halle- lu- jah, halle- lu-   jah
          G   D       D/C  C
Halle- lu-  jah, what a Sav- ior
    D     G   D       D/C  C
Halle- lu- jah, halle- lu-   jah
          G   D       D/C  C   Esus   E
Halle- lu-  jah, what a Sav- ior
```

VERSE 3
```
    A       A/C#      F#m7    E
When He comes, our glorious King
    D     A/C#    E/B  B E7sus   E
All His ransomed hearts to  bring
    A     A/C#  F#m7     D       A/E  E       E/D  D   E
Then a- new this song we'll sing, halle- lu-   jah, what a Sav- ior
```

CHORUS
```
    E    A   E      E/D  D
Halle- lu- jah, halle- lu-   jah
         A   E        D  D/F#  Bm7  A/C#   D
Halle- lu-  jah, what a Sav-          ior
   E/G# A   E      E/D  D
Hal- le- lu- jah, halle- lu-   jah
         A   E      E/D  D
Halle- lu-  jah, what a Sav- ior
```
(Repeat)

```
E/D  D  E/D  D  E/D  E  E/D  E  E/D  D
```
(Repeat as desired)

Your Word Will Be The Last Word (1 of 2)

Tommy Walker

VERSE1
```
      E  B/D#          A/C#   E/B   E/G#
Your Word will be the last word
A                E/G#  F#m7        B7sus    B
Your promises will stand      forevermore
         E              B/D#   G#7   B#dim7   C#m7   A2
Man's thoughts and all his plans will come to an end
           E/B  B7sus         A   B7sus
But Your Word       will be the last word
```

VERSE 2
```
B    E   B/D#        A/C#   E/B   E/G#
Your Word says I'm for- given
A               E/G#   F#m7            B7sus    B
Your covenant says You will always be with me
         E          B/D#   G#7   B#dim7   C#m7   A2
Though some may scoff and write me     off
     E/B  B7sus          A/E   E   C
Your Word will be the last word
```

VERSE 3
```
      F  C/E       Bb/D     F/C   F2/A
Your Word is my guid- ing light
Bb              F/A              Gm7      C7sus
Your promises guide me in the deepest, darkest night
             F         C/E      A7     C#dim7   Dm   Bb
Though troubles come and go in my heart I'll al- ways know
     F/C  C          Bb  Gm7   F
Your Word will be the last word
```

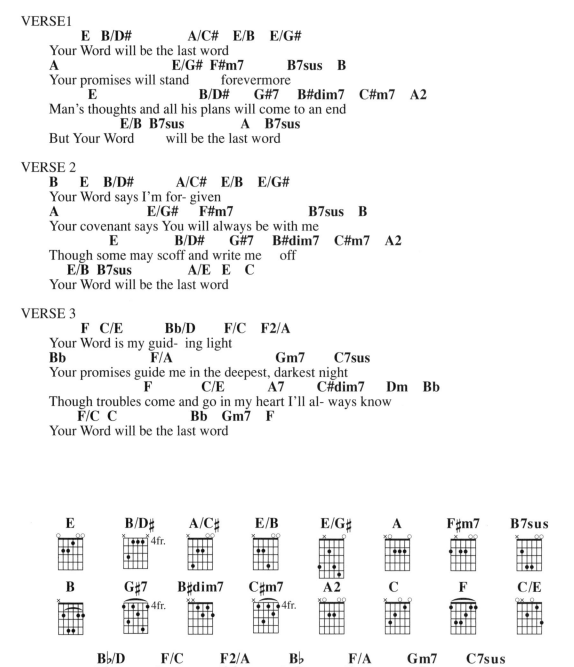

Your Word Will Be The Last Word (2 of 2)

BRIDGE
```
    C              A7/C#        Dm      A7     Dm
    Man in all his wis- dom and all his fool- ish pride
    Gm7            F/A                 Bbmaj7  G7/B     C  G/B
    Puts his hope in on- ly things he can see with      his eyes
    C              A7/C#        Dm      A7     Dm
    Claiming to be wise they became as fools in- stead
      Gm7            F/A              Bbmaj7  G7/B      C7sus   C#7sus
    But Lord I'm banking all my faith  on the truths of what You've said
```

VERSE 4
```
    C#7sus F# C#/E#          B/D#   F#/C#   F#/A#
    Your    Word    will be the last word
    B                 F#/A#  G#m7              C#7sus   C#
    Your promises will stand for- ever and ever and ever- more
      F#           C#/E#          A#7 Dm6  D#m7   B
    Man's thoughts and plans, they will come to    an end
          F#/C# C#           D#m   B
    But Your Word        will be the last word
          F#/C# C#          B  F#/A#  G#m7  C#7sus  F#
    Your Word       will be the last word
```

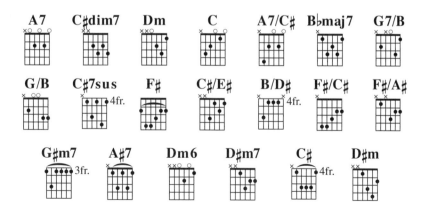

Prepare Ye The Way (1 of 3)

Tommy Walker

INTRO
    Gb   Abm7   Adim7   Gb7/Bb   Cbsus   Cb

    Ebm7   Abm7   Gb/Bb   Ab7/C   Cbm6
    (Repeat)

VERSE 1
        Gb Abm7   Adim7   Gb7/Bb   Cbsus   Cb   Ebm7
    Pre- pare ye   the   way for the Lord
    Abm7   Gb/Bb Ab7/C   Cbm6
    Make a highway   straight for our God
        Gb Abm7   Adim7   Gb7/Bb   Cbsus   Cb   Ebm7
    Pre- pare ye   the   way for the Lord
        Abm7   Gb/Bb Ab7/C   Cbm6
    Every valley raised up   and mountain made low
            Abm7   Abm7/Db   Gb   Abm7   Adim7   Gb7/Bb   Cbsus   Cb
    Let's make way in our hearts for the Lord
    Ebm7   Abm7   Gb/Bb   Ab7/C   Cbm6

VERSE 2
        Gb Abm7   Adim7   Gb7/Bb   Cbsus   Cb   Ebm7
    Pre- pare ye   the   way for the Lord
    Abm7   Gb/Bb Ab7/C   Cbm6
    Make a highway   straight for our God
        Gb Abm7   Adim7   Gb7/Bb   Cbsus   Cb   Ebm7
    Pre- pare ye   the   way for the Lord
    Abm7   Gb/Bb Ab7/C   Cbm6
    Turn from the dark and walk in the light
        Abm7   Abm7/Db   Gb
    Let's all make a way for the Lord

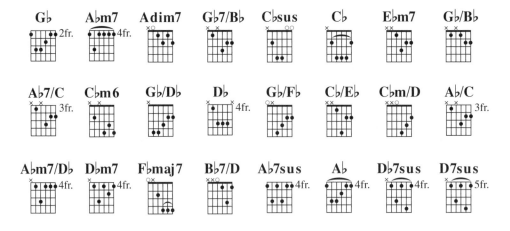

Prepare Ye The Way (2 of 3)

CHORUS
    Gb Abm7 Gb7/Bb   Cbsus Cb Ab7/C   Gb/Db Db
And His   glory will shine,   it will be shown to all mankind
    Gb/E   Cb/Eb Cbm/D   Gb/Db Ab/C
And we shall behold   our Savior come with His re- ward
  Cbm6   Abm7/Db   Gb Abm7 Adim7 Gb7/Bb Cbsus Cb
Prepare ye the way, make a way for the Lord
Ebm7 Abm7 Gb/Bb Ab7/C

BRIDGE
  Dbm7   Fbmaj7   Gb
Strengthen your weary hands and feet
  Dbm7   Fbmaj7   Gb
Walk on the path of holiness
  Abm7   Gb/Bb Cb   Db Bb7/D
Take heart and do not fear, our God will soon be here
  Ebm7   Ab7sus   Ab Gb/Db   Db7sus D7sus
And He'll crown our heads with ever- lasting songs of joy

VERSE 1
    G Am7 A#dim7 G7/B   Csus C Em7
Pre- pare ye   the   way for the Lord
Am7   G/B A7/C#   Cm6
Make a highway   straight for our God
    G Am7 A#dim7 G7/B   Csus C Em7
Pre- pare ye   the   way for the Lord
  Am7   G/B A7/C#   Cm6
Every valley raised up   and mountain made low
     Am7   Am7/D   G
Let's make way in our hearts for the Lord

CHORUS
  G Am7 G/B   Csus C A7/C#   G/D   D
And His   glory will shine,   it will be shown to all man- kind
    G/F   C/E   Cm/Eb   G/D   A/C#
And we shall behold   our Savior come with His re- ward
  Cm6   Am7/D   G Am7 A#dim7 G7/B Csus C Em7
Prepare ye the way, make a way for the Lord
Am7 G/B A7/C# Cm6

CODA
      G Am7 A#dim7 G7/B Csus C Em7 Am7 G/B A7/C# Cm6
Make a way,   way for the Lord
(Repeat)

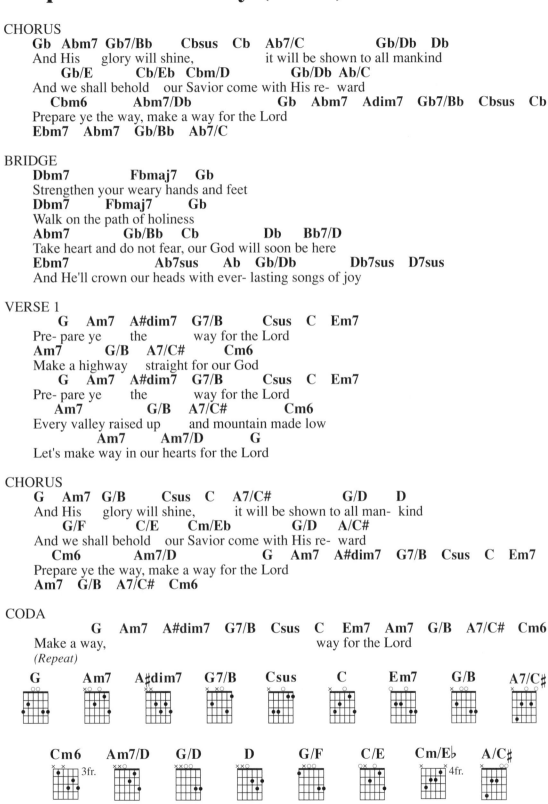

Prepare Ye The Way (3 of 3)

          Ab Bbm7 Bdim7 Ab7/C Dbsus   Db Fm7   Bbm7 Ab/C Bb7/D Dbm6

Make a way,   way for the Lord

(Repeat)

          A Bm7 B#dim7 A7/C# Dsus   D F#m7   Bm7 A/C# B7/D# Dm6

Make a way,   way for the Lord

(Repeat)

A   A7

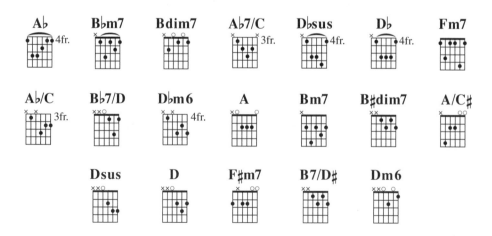

Overhead Masters

Prepare Ye The Way (1 of 2)

(Verse 1)
Prepare ye the way for the Lord
Make a highway straight for our God
Prepare ye the way for the Lord
Every valley raised up and mountain made low
Let's make way in our hearts for the Lord

(Verse 2)
Prepare ye the way for the Lord
Make a highway straight for our God
Prepare ye the way for the Lord
Turn from the dark and walk in the light
Let's all make a way for the Lord

(Chorus)
And His glory will shine
It will be shown to all mankind
And we shall behold our Savior come with His reward
Prepare ye the way, make a way for the Lord

Prepare Ye The Way (2 of 2)

(Bridge)
Strengthen your weary hands and feet
Walk on the path of holiness
Take heart and do not fear
Our God will soon be here
And He'll crown our heads
With everlasting songs of joy

Make a way
Way for the Lord
Make a way
Way for the Lord

Tommy Walker
© *1997 Doulos Publishing (adm by The Copyright Company, Nashville, TN)/BMI*

Make It Glorious

(Verse)
Make it glorious, Make it wonderful
The praises of our King
Make it passionate, Given from our hearts
Sing praises to our King
Make it excellent, Make it beautiful
The praises of our King
Let Him hear how much we really thank Him
Sing praises to our King

(Chorus)
Shout with joy
To our God
All the earth
Give glory to His name
He deserves nothing less
Than our hearts and souls
Our very best

Jesus We Celebrate Your Fame (1 of 2)

(Verse 1)
Jesus, Jesus, Jesus, Jesus
We celebrate Your fame
You are the only One Who bears
That name above all names
God made flesh, You came to earth
When a star announced Your glorious birth
You shed Your blood and then were raised
Now all Heaven sings Your praise

(Verse 2)
Jesus, Jesus, Jesus, Jesus
Now the nations sing Your song
Even now there's millions far and wide
Lifting up Your name on high

(Chorus)
Hallelujah, hallelujah
Hallelujah to the King
Hallelujah to our Savior
It's of His great fame we sing

Tommy Walker
© *2004 Integrity's Praise! Music/BMI*

Jesus We Celebrate Your Fame (2 of 2)

(Verse 3)
Jesus, Jesus, Jesus, Jesus
All history proclaims
The earth has never been the same
Since You showed the world Your grace

(Verse 4)
Jesus, Jesus, Jesus, Jesus
Soon every knee will bow
We'll crown You Lord and King of kings
And then all the world will sing

Tommy Walker
© 2004 Integrity's Praise! Music/BMI

Heavenly Touch (1 of 2)

(Verse 1)
Heaven's great mystery
How the God of eternity
Reaches down far from worlds unknown
To the human race
Making His love in us known

Heaven's great blessing received
Is a God full of mercy, so free
Reaching out throughout time and through space
To the human race
Revealing His peace and His grace

(Chorus)
O the wonder of His heavenly touch
Filled with such hope filled with such love
O the mystery how it reaches deep in me
Restoring my soul and making me ever whole

Tommy Walker
© 2004 Integrity's Praise! Music/BMI

Heavenly Touch (2 of 2)

(Verse 2)
Heaven's great history
Shows a God full of kindness and strength
Reigning down on the hardest of hearts
Piercing through all the dark
With healing and light from afar

Heaven's great gift to the earth
Was our Savior our Lord's humble birth
He came down from His throne up above
To be born here in us
Giving His unending love

(Bridge)
All I wanna do is thank You, Lord
All I wanna do is praise You, Lord
For touching me loving me and
Sending Your Spirit to set me free

Tommy Walker
© 2004 Integrity's Praise! Music/BMI

Thank You For Loving Me (1 of 2)

(Verse 1)
What love the Father has lavished on us
That we should be called His sons and daughters
Precious in His sight
Greater love this world had never seen
When He hung on that tree
O, why would He do such a thing
For dirty sinners like you and me

(Chorus)
O, God thank You for loving me
When on the cross You made history
Lord, You died for me
Forever my praise will go to Thee
O, God thank You for choosing me
To be Your child and bare Your name
O, Jesus I will never cease to sing Your praise

Tommy Walker
© *2003 We Mobile Music (adm by Integrity's Praise! Music)/BMI and Integrity's Praise! Music/BMI*

Thank You For Loving Me (2 of 2)

(Verse 2)
Your love is patient and humble and kind
It's greater then all my sin
It always protects and trusts and hopes
And will have no end
It's Your love that lifted me up from the depths
Set my feet on a solid rock with a firm place to stand
Lord, I always will trust in Your loving hand

(Bridge)
How wide, how long, how high, how deep
How endless is Your love for me

Thank You for loving me
Thank You for loving me
Thank You for loving me
Thank You for loving me

Tommy Walker
© *2003 We Mobile Music (adm by Integrity's Praise! Music)/BMI and Integrity's Praise! Music/BMI*

Just Worship

(Chorus)
Just worship, Lord, I worship You
Just want to honor You
How my heart longs for You

(Verse 1)
Just worship, that's all I want to do is worship
Give my heart and soul to You
To be lost in Your presence and found in Your love
Letting all things fade away
I set my eyes on things above
And just worship I bow before Your throne
And worship how my heart longs for You alone
To be lost in Your presence and found in Your love
Letting all things fade away
I set my eyes on things above

(Verse 2)
To just worship when I don't know what to do
I'll just worship casting all my cares on You
To be lost in Your presence and found in Your love
Letting all things fade away
I set my eyes on things above to just

All I wanna do
All I wanna do is worship You

Tommy Walker
© *2004 Integrity's Praise! Music/BMI*

This God He Is Our God

(Verse 1)
Who is the God Who said to the darkness
Let there be light and there was light
Who is the God Who made the heavens
The sun and moon the stars and sky
He is One Who's like no other
Omnipotent and O so wise
Invisible yet ever-present
He is the holy God Most High

(Chorus)
This God He is our God
Forevermore and evermore
He'll be our guiding light
From now until the end of time

(Verse 2)
This is the God Who came down from Heaven
Said let the children come to me
He healed the sick and walked on water
He conquered death to set us free
He is the One Who's always loved us
Even when we've walked away
It is His love that will ever hold us
Until the day we see His face

Hallelujah, hallelujah

Tommy Walker
© 2004 Integrity's Praise! Music/BMI

I'm Not Ashamed

(Verse 1)
I'm not ashamed of Your love
Not ashamed of Your grace
Not ashamed of the cross
Not ashamed of Your Word
From the highest mountain top
To the lowest valley low
I'll shout Your name until the
Whole world knows

(Chorus)
Jesus, You're my Master and my King
Jesus, You're my Lord, my everything
Jesus, it's Your blood that made me clean
Hallelujah, hallelujah

(Verse 2)
What can I do but dance and shout
I have to let these praises out
I once was lost and O so bound
By Your grace I have been found
And if the world can scream and shout
For earthly temporary things
I can give my loudest praise to Thee

(Bridge)
Hallelujah, hallelujah

Tommy Walker
© 2004 Integrity's Praise! Music/BMI

Lord I Run To You

(Verse 1)
Lord, I run to You
No one else will do
Lord, in troubled times I will run straight to You
Though my heart and flesh may fail
You're my ever present help
My tower of strength, my portion evermore

(Verse 2)
Lord, I run to You
No one else will do
Lord, You said we'd face trouble pain and fears
But to be of good cheer, be of good cheer
For You have overcome, overcome the world

(Chorus)
I lift my eyes up to the mountains
Where does my help come from
It comes from You, Lord
You are the Maker of earth and Heaven
And there is nothing that's too hard for You

Tommy Walker
© *2004 Integrity's Praise! Music/BMI*